Home Course in Religion

New Poems by Gary Soto

CHRONICLE BOOKS

San Francisco

CT   P91

Printed in the United States of America.

Library of Congress Cataloging-in-Publication Data

Soto, Gary.
    Home course in religion: new poems / Gary Soto.
        p.   cm.
    ISBN: 0-87701-857-X
    I. Title.
PS3569.O72H6   1991
811'.54—dc20   90-23015
                                                     CIP

Distributed in Canada by Raincoast Books,
112 East Third Avenue, Vancouver, B.C. V5T 1C8

1 2 3 4 5 6 7 8 9 10

CHRONICLE BOOKS
275 Fifth Street
San Francisco, California
9 4 1 0 3

Acknowledgements

Some of these poems first appeared in the
following magazines: *ARETE, CALIBAN,
CHRONICLE OF HIGHER EDUCATION, COLORADO
REVIEW, INDIANA REVIEW, THE NATION, NEW
AMERICAN WRITING, NEW CHICANO WRITING,
WITNESS*, and *ZYZZYVA*.

"Not Moving," "The Box Fan," and "The
Dictionaries" appeared in *POETRY*.

This book is for Christopher Buckley.

ONE ✦

Contents

TWO ✦

✦ One

PINK HANDS ·

I miss not eating fish on Friday,
The halved lemon squeezed a third time around,
And our prayers, silent mutters
To God, whom we knew, whom we trusted
To make things right. I miss the incense,
White scarf of smoke. I miss Monsignor Singleton
Saying Mass in Latin with his back to us.
When he raised the Host, I looked down,
Usually at my hands, which were pink like the underside
Of a starfish. I miss the nuns, and the chalk smells
Of popped erasers, and the peppery corduroy
That *swished* when we walked. I never understood
The Trinity, and still have doubts,
But was happy for the Father, Son, and Holy Ghost.
I miss Sister Maria, her white-dove skin,
And the pagan babies waiting for our candles.
My favorite country was Italy, the boot country.
The Pope lived there in his many robes,
And Venice was a flood of fishless canals.
This made me dream a lot. I wished my town
Were water, not dry lawns and thistly kids.
I also liked France, which was Catholic,
And England, which was not Catholic
But green and cool like the insides of trees.
I miss walking home in my Catholic clothes.
I miss crossing myself when an ambulance raced its siren.
At home a crucifix hung in almost every room,
Holy water in the cupboard behind the jam
And a box of pretzels. The Bible
Weighed less than our medical dictionary,
Where the dead lay with toes poking through white sheets.
Palm-leaf crosses withered in the kitchen window
For our Okie neighbors to look at in awe.

Okies are now the homeless, car salesmen,
And waitresses. The pagan babies are the simple poor,
The nuns in their sleds of black shadow

Women with skirts up to their knees.
Our school, condemned by the city, now creaks
With mice, not the polished shoes of Catholicism.
In school, I didn't mean to be bad.
I wrote I WILL NOT TALK BACK a lot of times
On the blackboard, and some of that dust
Worked into my soul. Now I'm quiet,
The telephone is quiet, my family
And the people I like best are quiet.
The nuns would be proud of me,
And so would Monsignor Singleton,
Who once begged me to please be quiet in the confessional.
But Monsignor, I can't help talking.
The Church is changed. We have folksy guitars
And an electric bass to thump our hearts, croissants
Instead of donuts, and three kinds of coffee,
Juice if you want. There are more lawyers
Than ever, doctors, teachers, and the educated
Looking for a way out. There are retreats,
Young Adult groups, spaghetti dinners
For parents without partners,
Five-mile runs for priests and nuns,
Lay ministry, fewer bingo nights, more poor people
Cuddling newspapers over warm grates of steam.
Monsignor, good priest who stared holiness
Into my body, the church on Pine Street is in trouble:
At the altar of Mary, we have electric bulbs,
Not candles, sitting in the votive cups.
You drop a quarter
Into the slot and a single bulb comes on.
With more quarters, with more sins notching the soul,
The altar lights up like a pinball machine.
How do we kneel and pray at such a place?
Monsignor, come back, with a holy sleight of hand,
With the smoke, the wavering flame,
The glow of the votive cup like a red taillight,
The teary melt of wax. ✦

THE GOLD CANNON ·

Grown-ups didn't know more than me
About the dead. I'd ask, Do you really have to stay
There? and they would say, It's up to God.
Now that Father was dead I wondered
About him a lot. He was there,
But also in heaven, as my grandmother said.
I wanted to ask, How can he be in two places?
But knew better. I would lower my eyes
And remember Father's favorite shirt hung
On a shovel two days before he died.

I thought about heaven in a different way
From other kids. At the cemetery there was a cannon,
And every time we drove through the cement
Gate, I would get on my knees in the back seat
Of our Chevy and peek at the gold-painted cannon.
I thought the last thing a dead person did
Was stick his head in the barrel. An angel
Would help give the neck a little twist,
And then you were really dead. There was one cannon,
Like one God, and graves rolled on a hill,
Then over that hill, then up again. ✦

THE DICTIONARIES ·

Disease happened overnight, just when you thought you
Were going to make the baseball team.
At the stove, Mother with steamed-up glasses
Said you couldn't count your chickens,
Then wiped her hands and set the medical dictionary
In my lap—ringworm and a Chinese boy
In the iron lung made me sit up.
On another page, a row of eyeballs,
Some pink, some red and droopy,
Some gray because one side of the boy was dead.
This was a new one to me. I closed the dictionary
And the next day at school I remembered
The boy, the eyeballs, a mouth with its cave of sores,
Ringworms and cancer. I licked my pencil
And did math on my fingers and was beginning
To think that maybe disease made me bad at math.
At home in my bedroom I looked up
And down my arms and thought about the dead.
Sometimes I would press a flashlight
Against my palm and scare myself
Because I could see the blood,
Bright as a red scarf. My brother would
Look at his blood and I would look at mine,
And both of us would eat all our food.
Just before Advent we started learning religion.
One morning Sister told us about the Trinity,
Then told us to draw pictures of them.
I got confused because I couldn't figure them out
And drew three gray crosses, one taller than the next.
Sister yelled at me, pinched my shoulder,
And that night I decided to look
In our Catholic dictionary to see
About the Trinity. It said,
The mystery whereby God, while being numerically one,
Exists in three divine Persons. I was perplexed
Because that was only one religious word.
On the same page there were fifteen others,
On the next page there were twelve,

And sooner or later I would have to know
Them all. Right below *Trinity* was *Triple Candlestick*,
Which was easy. I memorized:
A candlestick so formed that three separate
Candles arise from one base. At dinner
I told Mother about the Triple Candlestick,
Potato in mouth. She was proud,
She said, and the next day at school
I waited for Sister to ask about the Triple Candlestick.
But she said again, Now draw the Trinity,
Which I thought was something like
People inside each other
And was somehow like manners.
Sometimes you could act one way at a friend's house,
But at your grandmother's house you had to act
Another way. I drew three faces, one larger than the next,
All looking pretty happy
But not so happy that they were smiling
And showing their teeth. Sister licked a blue star
Of approval and let me monitor the bad boys at lunch.
At home, I felt light and holy.
I got the can of marbles
That Uncle got us after Father died,
And poured them on the floor in the empty bedroom.
With the sweep of my hand, the marbles jumped up the walls,
Ricocheted and clattered. My brother joined me,
Then my sister, and all of us went wild making the marbles
Jump. When mother came home, we stopped.
Before dinner I peeked at the medical dictionary,
Lung sitting in a white pan. After dinner I looked
At the Catholic dictionary. I knew *Triple Candlestick*
And *Trinity*. On the same page
Was *Tre Ore*. I went to bed saying
Over and over, A devotion commemorating
The three hours' agony of Christ
On the cross. This was second grade, winter,
A year of troubled math and disease,
God the Trinity, with bleeding palms and redemptive heart. ✦

APPLE ·

I open the orange photo album
And they're there, family in black and whites,
Off-color color prints. I like the one of
My brother, sister, and me standing by a car
Fender. We're like bushes set not quite straight
In the ground, thin and crooked, and we are shading
Our eyes in childish salutes. The shadow
Of our mother behind the camera
Is lean. The ground at our feet is sandy.
The houses behind us are white, rickety white
From thirty years of rain. I like this
Photograph, circa 1956. We were new
In our bodies and the people we loved were still alive.
My uncle had a Model-T that I tried to help
Get started. Instead of pushing, I pulled
From the front fender and was dragged up the alley,
The engine whirring warm air into my face. My uncle
Stopped, pulled me up, and swatted a cloud
Of dust from my pants. My brother
Was tricking me then, too.
He would say, Captain Kangaroo
Lives in that house,
And of course I would climb the brick steps and knock.
He would point, That kid said you were black,
And I would pick up the nearest rock.
I didn't catch on right away
That meanness was part of the family.
I kept going where people told me to go.
One day my mother sent me to Charlie's Market
For an apple pie, the kind in which one end peeks
From a sleeve of waxed paper. I gave Charlie
The fifteen cents. I started
Home staring at the end of the apple pie,
Little snout of sugary crust.
I wanted very badly to take one bite.
I walked slowly, thinking, Just one bite.

Mother would say, You had yours without asking
But you should wait next time.
She wouldn't be too mad. I worried
About the apple pie, walked slowly
Around the block the long way,
And when I couldn't stand it anymore,
I took a bite. A sugary flake fell from my mouth.
It was sweet. I took a second bite
And three lines worried my brow.
I took the pie out of the paper
Wrapper, and turned it the other way
So the eaten side didn't show.
But I kept walking around the block, a kid
Lost in a neighborly orbit, and staring
At the pie. Again I couldn't stand it.
My mouth opened when my hand
Forced the pie to my face.
Now both sides were ruined,
Chunks gone out. How could I say,
Mom, I don't know how it got that way.
I hid in a vacant lot
Behind a stack of greenish boards,
Companion to the scurry of red ants at my feet.
I don't remember ever getting up to go back home.

Laughter is another sin. How funny
To think I could eat from both ends
And get away with it. God *is* at least that voice
Inside us that says *yes* and *no*.
God said *no*, and I hid behind a stack
Of boards. God said *yes* when
I tried to help Uncle with his old black car
And didn't let me die under a dusty wheel.
It's been that way ever since. Yes
And no, never a maybe. Because of this,
I once tried to steal from Charlie's Market.

I stood at a tier of thirteen kinds of candy,
And I closed my hand around a Baby Ruth,
Then opened it very quickly
Because it was wrong. I was a boy,
No brighter than the penny
In my pocket. I closed my hand around
The candy again, then opened it.
God would know, my mother would know,
And certainly Charlie who was leaning his elbows
On the glass counter. I didn't see him watching.
My small eyes stared at the candy,
First temptation of the greedy tooth.
My hand opened and closed around the Baby Ruth
Several more times. I kept thinking
All I have to do is pick it up
And it'll be mine. ✦

SOME MYSTERIES ·

I was pretty holy by third grade. Mother could see that,
And could see that I had given up stealing butt-faced plums
And walking with Pepsi cans smashed onto my shoes.
Sundays, she gave me a quarter for
The wicker basket, smoothed my hair with water
And let me go. I sat in the front pew,
Among old Italian women hunched together
Like pigeons, happy because it was only a matter
Of time before Monsignor would say, We are sinners.
I would look at my shoes
And nod my head Yes. I recalled my sins.
Years before I tossed a hairbrush
Into my sister's panties. It was a game in our bedroom,
Doctor Doctor, and for me the hairbrush
Resembled a doctor's tool.
I opened her panties and said, This should help—buzzzzzz.
While we played Mother came in with her apron of chickens,
And said, Alex is having a party—
Alex the boy whose hand
Traveled both ways in the wringer/washer.
Sister and I were scared because we thought mother saw.
She didn't. She wrung her hands into the apron,
Said, Wash your faces. I went to the bathroom
And hurt myself with hot water—the handles of
The faucets were confusing. I couldn't see sister.
I held onto the tub and blinked until
My eyesight returned. I then saw the brush
Wagging in her panties as mother prodded us
To the car. Sometime between
Our house and Alex's house, between childhood
And her older years, she got it out, that and more.
In church I would remember my sins and smile,
Then feel bad for remembering such moments.
When Mass was over and the donuts eaten,
I often stood outside admiring the stained-glass windows
Breathing in light—the crucified Jesus

Was blood red at twenty to noon. I felt bad for Him
But much better when I turned away. I liked the walk home,
And liked when I passed the rectory: behind the thorny wall
Thumping sounds like a soccer ball,
Which made me wonder what our nuns did on weekends.
I would listen for a while, then leave,
Thinking that maybe this is what mystery was,
That you hear a *thump* and have to guess
What it is. I guessed a soccer ball
And saw Sister Marie running around the yard.
Monsignor's hands were pressed together in prayer,
His eyes like the floating eyes of the saints
On the church ceiling. I had a lot of ideas back then,
And liked to walk around. *Thump* was mystery,
A ball against the wall, and after Mass,
After the Host cleaned you up, a scoreless game. ✦

THE MUSIC AT HOME ·

Sometimes I stared at the marble-white Christ
On the nightstand. Monsignor Singleton
Had blessed Him in the rectory
And said good things about us when he learned
We kept holy water in a cupboard.
Sometimes I stared at the mirror nailed
To the closet door and tried to scare myself.
For a long time I believed the air inside jars was ill,
That if you didn't open them up slowly,
If you didn't hold them from your body,
You'd get sick. I thought a lot
About the jars when my mother and stepfather
Argued. Jim yelled that we were spoiled,
That we didn't pick up around the yard.
I thought about the jar, the evilness of air,
And tried to remember everything he said.
A tape recorder helped. When I was twelve
My brother's friend David and I saved enough money
To buy a cheap one from Long's Drugs.
The Beatles were popular. Still, their faces collapsed
Into an egg of light when they appeared
On Ed Sullivan—our stepfather had words
For men with long hair. Still, we saved our money.
We wanted to sing along to their records
To see what we sounded like. We sang
At his house because it was scary at mine.
Sometimes David and I would go inside for a ball or a mitt,
And Jim would shout from his chair,
What do you want? Other times we would look in
From the front window. We could see that he
Was drunk. His head was sinking into his chest,
Mouth open to gray teeth. David and I sang
At his house and laughed a lot because
We were louder than the Beatles. David wanted to be
All the Beatles. One day he was Ringo,
The next Paul, then John. I had to be George

Because David paid a dollar more
For the tape recorder. Later we
Didn't play records but sang into the microphone
Songs we learned at school. One time when
I took home the tape recorder,
Mom and Jim were arguing. I walked quickly
To my bedroom and closed the door. The mirror
Was scary at the edges. Christ was marble white
And hollow, an afternoon glow from the window
Fading at His feet. When I turned on
The tape recorder, David was singing
"I Want to Hold Your Hand." I rewound the tape
And recorded *My feet hurt.*
You don't give a shit. You'll never give
A shit. I work all day and your kids aren't happy with food.
You don't know a damn thing about my children
Mom said, *You don't know a damn thing*
About anything. You got rice on your face
You drunk fool. They said these things slowly
Because the battery was dying. I sat on
The edge of the bed and remembered
The air inside a closed jar. I couldn't understand them.
I played the argument over and over
Until their voices slurred to a crawl
And the tape recorder died on the word *face.* It took
Another battery to make David and me sing. ✦

BEST YEARS ·

My stepfather smoked and drank
In front of the TV. I gripped the chair,
And my younger brothers sucked the nostril holes
Of Tinker Toys. Everyone was scared back then, even Mom.
He said, Best years of your life.
I wanted to stick my hands in the box fan
When he said this. The fan was the color
Of water from a faucet, and I thought,
I want to hurt them. I looked at a Western
On the television. A soldier fell from a horse,
The other cocked his rifle. Indians
Are wild I thought back then,
And now believe they weren't wild enough,
Living on sweetgrass that had marched from the plains
All the way to the sea. The best years,
He said, and I thought of my brother and David,
How earlier they had pinned me to the ground.
And let Pinkie, David's homing pigeon,
Perch on my forehead, weight like a warm stone.
Sometimes you don't want to get up after
A brother has slapped you around,
But look skyward between branches of sycamore—
The pinpricks of stars, planes, end-of-the-world colors.

At home it was the best years of my life.
My stepfather was drunk. The fan was moving pages
Of the *TV Guide*. An iced tea was floating
Slivers of ice cubes. I got up to get a glass
Of water and at the sink touched my forehead,
The weight of pigeon still there.
I drank the water and watched ants
Smother a moist apricot pit on the counter—
A faint shadow of ants along the baseboard.
I wondered about them. Sometimes
I found them on my hand, just looking it seemed,
Just following the newish hairs on my knuckles.
Once I opened a library book and I found one there,
The black of a comma, shadow of the lower-case i.

When I returned more Indians were dying on TV.
My brothers had dropped their Tinker Toys
And were poking their wet fingers through the red
And orange afghan that covered the couch.
I returned to my chair. When my stepfather started
On Pearl Harbor, Nips mostly,
I gripped both arms and looked at the fan,
Its watery color, its whir of warm air.
I got up and sat next to my brothers.
I stuck my fingers through the afghan,
The flesh of nothing to do. We were scared,
The three of us, and when he said Nips
Should be dead, a TV Indian tumbled
From a cliff with a fist of smoke in his back.
The three of us looked at our fingers,
Smiled. I touched Jimmy's fingers
And laughed because it was something to do.
We stopped, though. Mom was pulling into the driveway
Back from Safeway. We went out to help,
Bags like boulders and one in each arm.
She made a face at my stepfather, the crushed beer
Cans on the TV tray, and he said, Japs.
I looked at the TV as I passed
From the living room to the kitchen.
A horse, head down,
Limped with its mouth full of grass.
Rick, my older brother and David's friend, came in,
Faces hot. He looked at me, laughed,
Said, "You better not tell."
I touched my forehead. I helped Mom with the groceries
—eggs mostly, bread and cans of tuna.
When I returned to the living room
The TV was off, the Indians were killed,
And the fan was low, less hurtful, less like water
Than a thing that goes around. I looked at my stepfather
Who was asleep, his glasses slipped down,
His work shirt sinking shadows into a hairy chest.

Best years. I climbed into my bunk bed
(three brothers to one room) to read a comic book,
The heroes bleeding ink on my fingers.
When Mom said it was time to sleep, my brothers
Undressed and climbed into their beds, blankets off.
I turned in the dark, breathing in and out,
Listening to the sounds our house made.
The refrigerator came on. A metal zipper clanged
In the dryer and the new wood creaked on its foundation.
I heard my stepfather get up from his La-Z-Boy
And walk into the kitchen to sit at the table.
Through the cracked door I saw Mom walk past him,
Her face spooked with a pinkish night cream.
She let water run cool from the kitchen sink.
She looked at my stepfather, her husband of six years,
Her one mistake. He looked up,
Eyes splayed red from drinking away a dead Sunday,
And said, You too. The best years of your life. ✦

AFTERNOON TOAST ·

The babysitter held a slice of bread
Over the stove burner, said, Ouch, Mary God.
We didn't have a toaster. Just bread and butter,
And a babysitter's hunger. Betty scared me.
For ten minutes she would watch TV,
Spitting ice cubes into a glass and then tilting the glass
So that they would fall back into her mouth.
The next ten minutes she would hold a slice over
The petals of blue flames,
The butter crawling from the center,
The corners sparking red and blackening just enough
To make it toast. That was morning,
Now it was afternoon, the heat moving
From one corner to the next.
Betty got up from the recliner, a drip of ice cube
On her chin. She made three slices,
Splotched with butter, and ran her fingers under the faucet.
At the kitchen table I drank from a blue aluminum tumbler,
One eye on the nickel-colored water,
The other straining to see if any moment a spark
Clinging to the toasts would leap into her hair.
I was playing Chinese checkers by myself. Debra
Was cutting paper skirts for her cardboard doll.
Rick was "drafting," as he called it, his left knee
Jerking up and down. I peeked at his lined paper,
The crumbs of pink eraser, and the drawing of a house
With three lions. Betty came over to look.
The toast was dead of sparks,
Her fingers cool when she ran them
On the back of my neck and asked me
Who was winning. I said the green marbles
But the red ones were catching up.
When she bit into the toast, black crumbs rained
Onto Rick's drawing. She bit two more times,
More crumbs and a single drop of water from her chin.
The refrigerator came on. A fly got in the way.

Rick blew the crumbs. He wasn't going to cry
Or poke an elbow into her wobbly stomach.
I only glanced up when she cleared her throat.
I only wet my lips when her buttery thumb touched my neck.
Debra got up, hugging her paper clothes,
The toy scissors on a thumb. I went outside
With a fistful of green marbles
And sat in the shade of a neighbor's tree.
I clicked two marbles together, and thought of ice,
Of water on a chin and toast in the back of the throat,
Of our working mother floating peeled potatoes in a trough.
I made a circle in the dust. When I looked up
Rick and Debra were like cut-out dolls holding hands,
Wavering on the front lawn. Betty was at the window —
An ice cube went in, then spilled back into the oily glass. ✦

THE BOX FAN ·

For nine months the box fan held its breath
In the closet. For three months of summer
It rattled the pages
Of *TV Guide.* It was summer now.
My stepfather was drinking Jack Daniels
From a TV tray pressed with the faces
Of our dead and live presidents.
The trouble with you,
He said, is that you don't respect the law.
He had come home from work, fingers black
From book print, the fissures of paper cuts
On the web of skin
Between thumb and index finger.
I had chained my bike to a tree.
He said there were laws against that kind
Of behavior. It hurt the tree. It was an eyesore.
Babies could poke an eye out on the handlebars
And could take away our house.

The sour heat of bourbon cracked the ice.
The pages rattled in the whir of the fan,
Blades the color of spoons and forks falling
From a drawer. I knew
It would take more than a knife to bring him down,
More than a slammed door to jam his heart.
You see my point? he said,
And then asked me to spell *implements,*
A word he picked up from *TV Guide.*
While I spelled the word,
While I counted out the letters
On my fingers, he drained his bourbon,
The sliver of ice riding the thick chute of throat.
He poured himself another and said,
I like that. I-m-p-l-e-m-e-n-t-s.
It's a good word to know.
He fixed the fan so that my hair stirred

And the pages of the magazine ruffled
From Sunday to Friday. I saw a serious face,
Then a laughing face in those pages,
Ads for steam cleaning and miracle products,
And the shuffle of my favorite nighttime shows.
He said that the trouble with me,
With a lot of young people, is that we can't spell.
He poured an inch of bourbon, with no ice,
And said, Try it again, without your fingers —
I imagined the fan blades and blood jumping to the wall. ✦

SOME WORRY·

In second grade I still had to stand far away
From the urinal to get my pee in.
This made me nervous. I opened myself up
To bacteria and dust swirling in the shafts of sunlight.
I worried more and more about disease.
I was still looking at the medical dictionary
And staring at the Chinese boy in
His iron lung. We became friends.
I would open the dictionary
And by habit the book fell open to his face.
I looked at him, and more than once I grew scared
Because I thought it was my face in the iron lung picture
And if I closed the book I might go away.
I worried about not feeling enough.
Sometimes when I prayed my shoulders tingled,
And other times I only felt the rub of cloth. Sister Marie
Said glorious things happened when boys and girls
Were sincere. I thought maybe I
Had forgotten to confess all my sins,
And thought maybe because some of my pee
Fell on the ground God was keeping me from feeling.
This scared me. Feeling was one of five senses,
And if you didn't feel that meant you only had
Four other senses and there was no telling
When you might go blind, or one of your best friends
Might shoot a cap gun in both your ears.
Of course I could cry. What I wanted to return
Was that tingle in my shoulders. For about eight years
I didn't feel too much, and worried a lot.
My eyesight was failing and sometimes I had difficulty
Hearing the teacher talk about the Euphrates.

One summer, when I was sixteen,
Feelings slowly came back to my shoulders
And my face began to turn red when relatives
Fumbled in their pockets for dimes
And said, Gary, you've grown tall. At first

I thought I was getting sick and became
Very suspicious of people who didn't wash their hands.
Then I realized I was becoming more in tune
With people. I got to thinking that maybe
This is how a saint feels when he's about
To do something really nice. By this time
I had stopped praying,
And the Christ in our bedroom began to glow
Later and later. But my feelings returned,
I got in the habit of
Walking around and singing
Made-up prayers. The trees seemed special.
The old Armenian neighbor took a long time
To wave but eventually he
Stopped his raking to raise a hand.
At school, my grades improved.
I was startled when I recognized a verb in a sentence
And began to think that maybe teachers were
Onto something after all. I would read,
The Euphrates, a mighty river that replenished
The Persian Empire time and time again,
Is a mile wide at more than twenty junctions.
Always when I got to the verb *is*,
My face burned a little and I became happy.
I realized learning was a bodily thing,
That you could read a really important book
And knowledge would spread into your face and your chest.
I began to walk slower in
The hallways, no longer embarrassed
About poor grades. I began to recognize the
Smart kids because none of them rushed around
A lot. Since I was now among them
This made me feel OK about myself. My shoulders tingled.
My face turned red for every class except algebra,
Which was still, $x = \dfrac{-b \pm \sqrt{b^2 - 4ac}}{2a}$

But by my senior year these feelings left me.
When I looked at a verb, my face didn't respond.
The words to prayers seemed silly,
And trees that were once special didn't move so much.
Once, in an abandoned house, I almost cried
Because the wallpaper was peeling,
And a really sad orange, blue from being forgotten,
Was on the floor and not even the ants bothered with it.
The Venetian blinds were the kind that hung
In our house on Braly Street,
And no matter how I pulled on the chain
I couldn't straighten them. The rooms were crooked
With shadows. The refrigerator blazed with flies
And the festering mold of peaches crawled in a cardboard box.
I went room to room strangling wire coat hangers.
Something was wrong. On my way back
Home, I realized that the Chinese boy
In the iron lung was dead. His lungs, vest of
Sorrow, were shredding apart in the black earth. ◆

A WAY OF THINKING ·

Nothing was wrong with me in fifth grade,
Inside or out. I felt good and clean
And lucky when one Sunday
I left nine o'clock Mass at St. John's
And saw a car door suddenly open.
A boy, maybe three, maybe five, fell out.
The father braked when the mother screamed,
Blue smoke from the back tires
And leaves from the gutter spiraling into the air.
The boy was only wide-eyed and scared.
Everything that was wrong with the boy
Was wrong with the mother. Both were crying
As they drove away, scattering leaves
In blue smoke. I thought, God wanted me to see this.
I walked home searching the street
For more leaves, a penny for the pagans,
Blinding glass, a voice in a paper cup.
God was talking to me. I drank water,
Said a prayer while standing by the stove,
And wanted to tell my brother
That I might never die. I felt very good,
Something like happy, because I could fall
From a car and be alright. I could spill a pitcher
Of grape Kool-Aid. I could be scolded
For not folding the laundry.
The boy who fell from the car was probably
Feeling better right now, and the mother was pouring
Coffee for her husband and feeling tired
But OK. I was feeling OK. I didn't spill the pitcher
And no one was home at the moment to scold me
So that later I could feel better. I ate oranges
In the backyard and played with my dog—
Twilight lived in her eyes,
An itch marched from her orange shoulder
To a white paw. I climbed the fence
And in the alley Little John, a Catholic friend,

Was feeling awful.
He said he'd broken his mother's yardstick —
Placed between two chairs,
It snapped when he jumped. I said,
That's not bad, and said that it was better
To get hit because he would feel awful,
Then later happy. His eyes filled.
He wiped his nose and together
We walked up the alley. The sky was scratched
With a lot of clouds. Birds flittered from fence posts.
We turned from the alley onto Angus Street
And stared at a leaf fire smoldering
The evil coals of things that break down and die.
We went as far as Jefferson Elementary,
Where we watched three boys burn candy wrappers.
We then returned to our neighborhood.
Little John was scared. He didn't want me to go home.
I said it was OK.
His mother would yell
And hit him once across his arm, scream that
It was lucky for him she kept a second yardstick
In the pantry. He turned away with tears
In his eyes, and there, standing in his dirt drive,
I realized that you can cry before anything happens
And thought that maybe this was Catholic.
When I heard a chair turn over and Little John
Screaming, I walked away. He was feeling awful now
But later he would be happy. Dinner was at 5:45 —
Spaghetti piled to his throat, string beans,
An Italian father's hands tearing up the bread, first. ✦

SATURDAY AT THE CANAL ·

I was hoping to be happy by seventeen.
School was a sharp check mark in the roll book,
An obnoxious tuba playing at noon because our team
Was going to win at night. The teachers were
Too close to dying to understand. The hallways
Stank of poor grades and unwashed hair. Thus,
A friend and I sat watching the water on Saturday,
Neither of us talking much, just warming ourselves
By hurling large rocks at the dusty ground
And feeling awful because San Francisco was a postcard
On a bedroom wall. We wanted to go there,
Hitchhike under the last migrating birds
And be with people who knew more than three chords
On a guitar. We didn't drink or smoke,
But our hair was shoulder length, wild when
The wind picked up and the shadows of
This loneliness gripped loose dirt. By bus or car,
By the sway of train over a long bridge,
We wanted to get out. The years froze
As we sat on the bank. Our eyes followed the water,
White-tipped but dark underneath, racing out of town. ✦

FALL AND SPRING ·

For years I thought it was better to sit
Around the house than to get in the car and drive.
When I first drove in my senior year it was scary but fun.
My parents were at work, and our second car, a Rambler,
Is what I took out during lunch. They didn't know.
No one knew. I thought it was pretty smart to drive
With one hand on the wheel and the other on a sandwich.
I thought it was pretty weird to steer
With my eyes closed, just for a few seconds,
Just for three or four houses before I opened
Them and had strange feelings around my eyes.
It was best in fall. Leaves scattered
And mixed with the smoke from the tailpipe.
I laughed a lot when I looked in the rearview mirror.
The leaves were leaping, and the block
Was pulling away, blue at the edges.
Sometimes when I started off
Flies gripped the hood. I would laugh,
Put the car into gear and
Say, Hang on, bugs.
At thirty the flies were usually pulled off by speed,
Which I knew to be like gravity, except sideways.
One time when a fly wouldn't come off,
I got the Rambler to fifty on Belmont, then braked
With both feet. I hit my head against the steering wheel
And laughed. I drove home
With no hands but used my thumbs to turn the
Corner onto Grant. My senior year I drove during lunch,
Then returned to school on foot. I didn't learn much.
I liked some of the girls. I wanted to tell them
About the Rambler but I didn't know if it was OK
To tell them because back then I thought girls
Were like teachers. I thought about girls a lot.
I often wondered about their houses.

I knew some of them
Had swimming pools. When I found out
Where June lived, I took the Rambler during lunch
And drove past her house. She was at school
Of course, but I liked driving slowly up and down
Her block and laughing. It meant
Something that she had a palm tree like ours
In her front yard. When I returned to school
I told her I knew that she had a palm tree
And sort of laughed, waiting for her to say
Something back. In math I realized it wasn't the kind
Of thing you say to a girl with a pool.

That spring Scott got his own car, a Ford Galaxy,
And I was happy to drive to the levee and stare
At the water. About then I began saying things like,
Scott, I think I lived before. Or, Scotty,
I have feelings around my eyes like I'm Chinese.
He let me say these things
And still be his friend. He told me
That his father was dead. I ran sand through my fingers.
I told him that when my father died
My uncle heard gravel crunch in the path
That ran along our house, and rock was one of
The things God told us to look out for.
The two of us ran a mile of sand
Through our fingers. We stared at the water,
Green rush that hissed over the reeds.
Saturday was the best for us. If we had a dollar,
We would drive pretty far. The levee was one place
But Sanger, a town outside Fresno,
Had a dairy where you could buy an icy bottle of milk
And look at the cows look at the grass.
We liked driving through Sanger. People stayed

In their houses. One Saturday was especially quiet.
No one bothered us when we got the Galaxy
Up pretty fast, braked, and laughed
Because we had to brace our arms on the windshield.
We liked that. We liked parking the car
And lowering ourselves into the seat,
Eyes straight ahead, and sayings things like,
It doesn't matter if we die . . . I have strange feelings
Around my eyes. Scott, a real friend,
Wasn't tired of hearing this. It was something to say.
I told him about June's palm tree.
He said he thought it was pretty weird,
That it was like a girl he liked in seventh grade
Having the same house numbers as his house.
Scott then said, My father is dead.
I said, Mine too. Blossoms ruined themselves
By falling from black branches. People
Stayed closed in their houses. He started the car
And, laughing, braked at the end of the street
As hard as he could without our dying. ✦

THE WRESTLER'S HEART ·

I had no choice but to shave my hair
And wrestle—thirty guys humping one another
On a mat. I didn't like high school.
There were no classes in archeology,
And the girls were too much like flowers
To bother with them. My brother, I think,
Was a hippie, and my sister, I know,
Was the runner-up queen of the Latin American Club.
When I saw her in the cafeteria, waved
And said things like, Debbie, is it your turn
To do the dishes tonight? she would smile and
Make real scary eyes. When I saw my brother
In his long hair and sissy bell-bottom pants,
He would look through me at a little snotty
Piece of gum on the ground. Neither of them
Liked me. So I sided with the wrestling coach,
The same person who taught you how to drive.
But first there was wrestling, young dudes
In a steamy room, and coach with his silver whistle,
His clipboard, his pencil behind his clubbed ear.
I was no good. Everyone was better
Than me. Everyone was larger
In the showers, their cocks like heavy wrenches,
Their hair like the scribbling of a mad child.
I would lather as best I could to hide
What I didn't have, then walk home
In the dark. When we wrestled
Madera High, I was pinned in twelve seconds.
My Mom threw me a half stick of gum
From the bleachers. She shouted, It's Juicy Fruit!
And I just looked at her. I looked at
The three spectators, all crunching corn nuts,
Their faces like punched-in paper bags.
We lost that night. The next day in Biology
I chewed my half stick of Juicy Fruit
And thought about what can go wrong

In twelve seconds. The guy who pinned
Me was named Bloodworth, a meaningful name.
That night I asked Mom what our name meant in Spanish.
She stirred crackling *papas* and said it meant Mexican.
I asked her what was the worst thing that happened
To her in the shortest period
Of time. She looked at my stepfather's chair
And told me to take out the garbage.
That year I gained weight, lost weight,
And lost more matches, nearly all by pins.
I wore my arm in a sling when
I got blood poisoning from a dirty fingernail.
I liked that. I liked being hurt. I even went as far
As limping, which I thought would attract girls.

One day at lunch the counselor called me to his office.
I killed my sandwich in three bites. In his
Office of unwashed coffee mugs,
He asked what I wanted from life.
I told him I wanted to be an archeologist,
And if not that, then an oceanographer.
I told him I had these feelings
I was Chinese, that I had lived before
And was going to live again. He told me
To get a drink of water and that by fifth period
I should reconsider what I was saying.
I studied some, dated once, ate the same sandwich
Until it was spring in most of the trees
That circled the campus, and wrestling was over.
Then school was over. That summer I mowed lawns,
Picked grapes, and rode my bike
Up and down my block because it was good
For heart and legs. The next year I took Driver's Ed.
Coach was the teacher. He said, Don't be scared
But you're going to see some punks
Getting killed. If you're going to cry,

Do it later. He turned on the projector,
A funnel of silver light that showed motes of dust,
Then six seconds of car wreck from different angles.
The narrator with a wrestler's haircut came on.
His face was thick like a canned ham
Sliding onto a platter. He held up a black tennis shoe.
He said, The boy who wore this sneaker is dead.
Two girls cried. Three boys laughed.
Coach smiled and slapped the clipboard
Against his leg, kind of hard.
With one year of wrestling behind me,
I barely peeked but thought,
Six seconds for the kid with the sneakers,
Twelve seconds for Bloodworth to throw me on my back.
Tough luck in half the time. ✦

THE LEVEE ·

At seventeen, I liked driving around,
Breaking the backs of leaves and casting long shadows
Where the lawns were burned. I didn't like home,
Especially in summer. But eventually I returned to watch
My stepfather eat fried chicken on a TV tray.
He ate for bulk, not taste,
And every night he drank to flood the hole inside him.
I couldn't believe my life. I was a Mexican
Among relatives with loud furniture. I knew most
Of us wouldn't get good jobs, some
Would die, others pull over
On the sides of roads to fix their Nova Super Sports
For a hundred years. I wanted out
Because the TV wouldn't stop until eleven.
The summer heat billowed near the ceiling.
Flies mingled among the smells
Of pried-apart chicken wings. I sweat
When I drank water from a dirty glass. I thought of
Putting my fingers in the box fan, of standing up
Nails under the tires of our neighbor's car.
That's why at night I drove to the levee
And played the radio. The water
Was constant, and the blown tires that bumped along
On a filthy current no longer surprised me.
The bushes breathed dust and hamburger wrappers,
The faint stink of dead birds. After a while
I talked to myself because the songs on the radio
Didn't seem honest. I was tired of home,
Of our TV wreathed in dollies
And the glow-in-the-night Christ on the windowsill.
I was sickened by the sound of toads flopping
In the dark, of a dying fish gasping among reeds.
I began to realize that we deserved each other,
Son to his stepfather, daughter to her real mother,
That it would take more than a car to make us happy.
We deserved this life, where a canal rushed
Black water, and the stars held for a while,
Then washed away as tires floated by in twos. ✦

SCHOOL NIGHT ·

Scott and I laughed. We thought it might
Be illegal to park in front of a teacher's house
And rock our Galaxy Ford. Nothing was happening inside.
The TV colored the walls, mostly purple.
Maybe our teacher was asleep in a La-Z-Boy recliner.
Maybe she was eating popcorn—another kerchiefed cowboy
Falling off a saloon roof on "Gunsmoke."
We stayed an hour, just looking, just rocking the car,
And then drove to the levee.
Scott said he couldn't believe he was seventeen
And how next year he could be in the army.
Feelings like radio waves circled my eyes.
Someone was communicating with me, I said,
And said, The more you suffer, the smarter you get.
Scott said, Only a bayonet could kill me.
Bedroom dust was pieces of another universe,
I said. Neither one of us
Believed in hell, and neither believed
In good grades. We both agreed that Mrs. Tuttle
Was a nice person, and, Scott first,
Said that we were sorry for parking in front of her house
And thinking weird thoughts about her La-Z-Boy recliner.
Bedroom dust carried disease, I said,
And Scott said, I ran away once
But they got me back. We stared
At the angry rush of black water over bacteria and weed,
And drove to a phone booth to look up
Mrs. McClosky's address. She was the Biology teacher
Who made a pretty girl kiss a petri dish.
Three days later, fungus toppled
Over the sides. The class made jokes
From fall to spring. Now was now. We drove wildly
To her house on a road of splattered cats
And broken-backed leaves. Nothing was happening
Inside us. Yet it was only quarter to ten.
Yet the needle glowed half-empty. At every chance,
We braked as hard as we could, eyes closed
And laughing. What could hurt us but ourselves? ✦

IN SUMMER ·

Girls left Scott and me alone. On Friday nights
Our happiness was taking corners very sharply
And laughing. We threw bottles from the car
And laughed even more. I didn't like driving in circles,
But in summer it was either that
Or sitting on the canal levee running
Miles of sand through our fingers.
We swam there during the day, or swung on a rope.
The water, swift and white
Where car fenders poked, was dangerous.
We swung on the rope and laughed.
We punched each other in the arm because
It was something to do. But Friday nights
We drove around, then parked the car,
The needle glowing above empty,
And walked tree-lined neighborhoods,
The blue faces of TV showing in living rooms.
It was possible then to think about the world,
To say things like, Russians have cooler
Veins because they're taller. Often at the canal
While I was swinging over the water,
I had odd feelings around my eyes
That I was Chinese and had lived before.
At home I checked the bathroom mirror,
Round-eyed and worried. When I smiled,
My eyes narrowed into slants—mountain wind had blown
In my face for a thousand years.
On our front lawns after dinner, I pulled up grass
And tried to explain to Scott what I felt on the rope.
Scott confessed he wanted to throw himself
Into the plate glass window
And make his mother pick up the pieces.
That summer we drove, then walked.
Three times I was lucky enough to sit

In the grass of Woodward Park and talk with girls
Who sucked on stalks of grass and worried
About the feelings around their eyes.
Life's weird, I thought,
But the girls were more than weird.
All three laughed when they saw falling stars,
Cracked up, and pulled up the grass crazily.
I was lucky. The last girl fanned the gnats
And let me kiss her, warm air
From a wet mouth. Later when I dropped her off,
I had to walk to make myself feel tired,
And once tired climb into bed. My older brother
Had already moved out of the house.
My younger brother, nearly asleep, could only say Oh
When I told him the warm air a girl breathes
On you makes a guy thirsty. He said Oh
And went to sleep. The next day it was cereal
For breakfast, some TV, some cards with my brother,
Then Scott in cut-offs at the door.
We drove to the canal and swung for an hour,
Our feet dragging in the cool water.
We didn't talk much. Leaves spun from the tree
And floated away. The sun gleamed
On the four corners of Scott's Ford Galaxy.
We watched others swing at funny heights on the rope,
And drag their feet in the canal.
I began to think that maybe we were the same —
A rope over water for guys,
Shooting stars for girls. That night, a Friday,
We drove around corners sharply. On the floorboard,
The music of bottles clinking against each other.
I told Scott that the bottles sounded weird
And he said Yeah a lot of times
And drove with one hand. Because it was something

To hear, I let the bottles roll.
I began to have feelings around my eyes,
Something like I was Chinese, something like I
Had lived before and was going to live again.
I said these things to Scott, who said Yeah
And pulled the car sharply around a corner.
His mouth pulled sharply as well,
Something like a sneer, and I thought,
I know that feeling but from where?
I told Scott about his mouth, and he said Yeah.
I said Yeah, and we drove until the car was empty
Of feelings and siphoned gas. ✦

DRINKING IN THE SIXTIES ·

Drinking made you popular at school,
And laughing while you drank
Made you friends. I noticed teachers
Laughed when they carried armfuls of books.
I began to think that they were drunk.
I noticed Mrs. Tuttle seldom kept her legs together,
Lipstick overrunning her mouth. Coach knew only
So many words. The dean's hand trembled
When he tried to open doors. Our English teacher
Kept repeating, A noun is a person, place, or thing.
You students are a noun, Fresno is a noun.
Bobbie's chair is a noun. Cheerleaders
Were pretty happy when thrown into the air.
Scott and I got a brown quart of beer
And sat in an abandoned house at dusk—
The walls were kicked open to chalk
Where rednecks banged heads.
We kept peering out the broken front window
And saying things like, Fuckin' narcs,
When we heard faraway voices. I sucked the old air
Of peeling wallpaper
And swigged beer with one eye on Scott.
I told him about the Chinese boy in the iron lung—
Vest of blood, milky skin of nothing to do.
You can live that way, with a hand mirror
To look around corners.
Scott swigged the quart and said,
Some rivers peter out before they get to the sea.
I swigged the quart and said that people
With long hair don't laugh as hard—
Except if they're a woman or a clean-cut hippie.
I walked to the window, cursed, Fuckin' queers,
And Scott with all his strength bent a wire hanger.
I liked the shape it took, and beat a board
Against the wall, chalky dust smothering the good air.
Scott kicked a greenish orange, dead of all sweetness,

Of rain and the bitter seeds.
I kicked the stove. I pulled a calendar from
The kitchen wall. The couch didn't mean
Much when slashed with a screwdriver.
We trashed that already trashed house,
And then we were sorry. Scott's hands
Were black. My armpits flooded with worry
And sweat. I slammed the quart, and thought of school:
Mrs. Tuttle's thighs and the cheerleaders cartwheeling
For a last-place team. Coach was farting softly
Into his bedsheets,
And the dean's hand was on the throat
Of his stinky dog. His wife smelled. His house was
Festering in lousy paint. Scott kicked the
Living room walls, and because I was seventeen
And acne bit my throat in three places,
I brought chair down on chair—
Splinters of wood flying at the windows.
Outside, we threw ourselves on a grave of leaves,
Groaning under the chipped moon's laughter. ✦

SPELLING WORDS AT THE TABLE ·

My stepfather held onto the wall,
Drunk and thanking God my hair was short—
My scalp the pink of a scar, the illness of an eye.
He knew only so many words. One night the word
Was *implements*. We practiced in the kitchen,
He with more beer, me with a coloring book
Of extinct birds. It was hard to get away—
Elbow raking across the table,
And the pounding of fists that pounded boxes all day.
The table wobbled and the metal screws
That held the Formica top to the legs
Loosened. He was a heavy man
While he talked. He had words for blacks,
Stalin, the yellow race that could jump up and down
And destroy us all. While he talked
I kept my hands under the table
And tightened the screws I could reach.
I was scared the table would collapse—
The salt shaker would rain its bad luck on the floor
And Mother would crumble her face into
Her apron of butchered flowers.

When he didn't come home from work,
I sometimes pressed an ear to the table,
My fingers on the screws. I listened to faraway sounds,
The just-dead howling through strata of rock?
Brother was on the couch with his fingers of nothing-to-do,
Mother was polishing the chrome coffeepot,
Flap of skin wobbling under her bluish chin.
It was scary at home. I tightened the already tight screws.
I had done everything to keep him home—
Spell, cut my hair, and, staying inside the lines,
Color extinct birds, in flight. ✦

✦ Two

NOT MOVING ·

Sometimes I would stub my toe on our La-Z-Boy recliner,
And mother, at her ironing board,
Sprinkling fingers of water from a saucepan,
Would say, God punished you. Scissors fell,
Splayed with angry light, and nicked my calf.
Mother was at the sink stirring the mush of
Starch for blue work shirts with black under the arms.
God punished you, she said, not looking up,
Not reaching for a towel.
My bike kicked up dirt when I fell,
And again I was punished—the bitterness of a rosebush
Biting through skin. Mother rolled down her
Window of our Dodge. God is making you pay, she said,
And then said, I'm going to buy milk.
The Dodge pulled away, stirring up the evil dust
Of leaves that won't die through any kind of rain,
And I walked home for circle Band-Aids. My brother
Stood under a tree and a pine cone fell
From a tree and ruined his eye for three weeks.
A screwdriver punctured his leg. Scalding water splashed
His foot. Spiders crawled into a pant leg,
Bites like braille he scratched
At night. Mother woke and stood in the doorway
With her cream of white medicine.
God punished, she said. It's time to eat.
Our ill luck couldn't stop our playing.
Cats dropped from roofs and lived.
Kids did the same, rolling like bales of hay,
And laughing with flakes of grass in their spiky hair.
I did the same,
And for one summer I had to sit on a porch—
My leg was hurt from the jump. My eyes as well.
I stared into a fan and everything dried
That makes the eyeball work.

Now I don't move so fast. I read in one room,
Eat in another. The front window is dust
With a geranium bush that wags against the glass—
Unlike the rose, its petals don't bite.
The scissors are sheathed in an oily cloth.
The screwdriver hangs on a wall.
Mother is in another town,
With her fingers still dipping into a saucepan,
Her iron pouting steam and hatred for collars.
Of course, God is here, at the level of trees,
At this hour of gnats circling bruised fruit on a limb.
His beard is long and the story the same.
I'm not moving from this chair,
From this life that could pick up a hammer
And hurt on the third strike. ✦

HOME COURSE IN RELIGION ·

By the time I was eighteen and in junior college
Religion was something like this: *The notion*
Of "project" is an ambiguous substitute for the notion
Of quiddity, and that situation is
An ambiguous substitute for the notion of an
Objective condition resulting from the causes
And natures interacting in the world. That was
The first sentence in a really long book.
I figured that the second sentence had
To be more difficult, and the third almost impossible,
On and on. The back of the book had impressive
Things to say. The author, a French scholar,
Got the Pope to say a few words, and one cardinal
I had heard about remarked, *Celebrated thought.*
Best Sellers said, *It ought to be read by anyone*
Who has had a formal or home-study course in metaphysics . . .
I read a chapter, then played basketball to get air
Back into my brain so I wouldn't feel so sleepy.
I returned home, sweaty in every hole,
And picked up a book that sounded like this:
Costly grace confronts us as a gracious call
To follow Jesus; it comes as a word of
Forgiveness to the broken spirit
And the contrite heart. This was clearer,
But after ten pages the good air in my brain was used up,
And I fell asleep with cracker crumbs
On my mouth. That night
My brother and I, and our two roommates, ate Top Ramen.
After dinner we tape recorded our thoughts
About Nixon, who was in a lot of trouble with Watergate.
We played it back and laughed for a long time
Because none of us understood what the other
Was saying. Some of it sounded like this:

Nixon won't confess
About the submarines or the money. Did you see how
He picked up that dog by its ears? No, that
Was Johnson. That's not the point. The certainty
Of life comes to an end. That Nixon!
People with big cars don't know how much it hurts.
Furthermore, if you realize the predicament
Then what's there to say, etc.

In bed I read four pages about a French mystic,
Who lived a common life until lightning struck
Her shoulder, then she began to talk in weird
Ways and no longer reached people with her thoughts.
The next morning I ate cereal
In my Top Ramen bowl. During P.E.
I understood more about life than with the help
Of a book. My karate instructor said,
Pain doesn't exist. Do you see
Pain when you get hit? Pain is in the mind.
The mind is the spiritual nature
That follows your body, etc. Then he matched us
By height and rank, and for twenty minutes
Let us kick and punch one another really hard.
By the time I got back to the apartment I thought
My instructor was wrong. With my one good eye
I could see the pain: red welts on my chest,
And two on my back from running away.

The Bible was much clearer. Jesus said,
O faithless and perverse generation, how long
Am I to be with you and bear with you? Bring
Your son here. Then I started on my roommate's book
About the Zen master Xu Yun. I was curious how
He could go three years eating only grass

And pine needles. I asked that about myself,
Seeing that I was living on Top Ramen and cold cereal
And oranges that rolled our way when we weren't looking.
That night my girlfriend came
Over with a large jar of peanut butter,
A present that we tried on our last three crackers.
After she left I prayed in my bedroom,
Then crossed myself so that my fingertips
Pushed into my flesh. I then started *The Problem of Evil*,
Which was clearer than my previous readings
Except when I ran into passages like this:
Oderunt peccare mali formidine poenae, oderunt peccare
Boni virtutis amore. I read nine pages
Before I fell asleep. The next morning
While I ate cereal from my Top Ramen bowl
I read a paragraph that said this: *Animal suffering?*
Their rate of production demands the existence
Of carnivorousness. But they are not dissatisfied
With life. They do not realize that they
Are suffering, they simply suffer, etc.
In Anthropology, I learned about the Papuan people.
In Geography, we discussed the use of pumice.
I took notes but mostly watched the teacher,
Sweat stinking up his eyebrows.

When Mom called to yell at us that night,
I told her that Rick and I were three years short
Of earning good money. She said that as long
As we didn't go to prison she would be
Proud of us. Prison wasn't what I was thinking,
And God knows what I was thinking
When I picked up the book *What Is Man?*
I had to keep looking at the cover to remind me

What I was reading. Some more good air
Left my brain, and I woke only when
My girlfriend came over with a bag of oranges.
We sat on the couch. Her blouse held a lot
Of shadows, and one was my hand. I liked
That very much, and liked how her mouth fit mine.
She said that she was lonely
When I wasn't around. I said that people feel
Like that because they don't know themselves.
I said just be mellow, just think of
Yourself as a flower, etc.
When I placed my hand on her thigh, she opened her legs
Just a little, warmth that was a spooky liquid
When one of my biggest fingers crawled in.
She pushed me away, lipstick overrunning her mouth,
Her hair like the hair you wear when
You wake up from a hard sleep. After she left,
I read in the Bible
About Jesus touching each of his four wounds—
Thomas was not around when Jesus walked through the wall.
I began to feel ashamed because my left hand
Turning the pages was the hand that had snapped
Her panties closed. I got up from the couch
And washed that hand, stinky trout that I took to bed.
It was then, on a night of
More Top Ramen and a cat-and-dog storm,
That I realized I might be in the wrong line of belief. ◆

THE HISTORY OF KARATE ·

Our sensei, Hiro N., scares me. Karate
Is a kidney shot to your wife's lover, not a bow
Or meditation or students crawling
In reverence, saying *Sensei, Sensei.*
He doesn't like Koreans and doesn't think much
Of us—Eurasian, Mexican, Berkeley women
With tattoos, three Japanese sissy boys.
We sit cross-legged against the wall
Asking questions about karate, questions like:
Is it possible to kill a bull with your eyes closed?
What if it hurts breaking ice with my head?
Should we pray before we eat
And bathe in cold-water streams? He tells us
To shut up. He reminds us how he practiced on snow,
Not on wooden floors. He points to the floor.
"This is nice. And this and this." He points
To the overhead lights, the mirrors,
The punching bag still dented from one of his kicks.
Earlier tonight, while we stretched
And jumped up and down to warm up, he pulled
A sword—a *katana*—from a sheath, swung it once,
Downward, and let his eyes go wild.
I was scared. My daughter is only nine
I thought, and my car payments three months old.
Worry rippled a leaf on my forehead,
Then vanished when Sensei put down the sword
And said to get our sparring gear.
Sensei is a family man, a good man.
He punches the women *karateka* with his left
Hand, not his right, which is terrible,
Like a car falling on your chest.

A lot of goons practice karate in Japan.
When student demonstrations take place on campus,
The *yakuza* and the martial arts clubs—*shorinji kempo,*
Shotokan, judo, and *aikido,* that palsy-walsy

Martial art—go out and make the students bleed
Very badly. Karate is right wing, protector
Of the state, and a good workout.
If you join a university club, you can never
Quit. You may say, "I'm bored,"
And they say, "You are not bored."
You can say, "Yes, I am really very bored,"
And they say, "No, you look happy."
This goes on for twenty minutes,
Maybe in your car, at a street corner,
In your dorm, before they bust you a couple of times.
Suddenly you're not bored in the least.
You are happy. You stay with the club. Later
When you graduate, you get a good job
Near the commuter line. Your wife does what you want.
The family is proud that you did push-ups in your youth
And hit a demonstrator so hard his eye
Is now flowery, like the inside of a marble.
They can now eat fish
And sleep in rooms with coals piled high.

A Ph.D. student did research on why older men
Take up karate. They have nothing else to do,
Are often stupid, were abused as kids.
Bullies pushed them to the ground
And told them to stay there.
Their tears froze and their arms turned blue
From the cold. The fast girls
Turned away. The male teachers fiddled
With their asses in doorways,
Oblivious to the playground scene. Before you knew it
The kids on the ground were in high school,
Wimps in the middle rows learning about
The Euphrates: millions along its shore
And only so much of the water crawling to the sea.
The grown-up kids who were on the ground

Suffer in their houses. But so do the bullies
Who have put on weight, rings of fat
That cast remarkable shadows over their crotches.
Some go to jail, some die, and others
Cut beef for a living, drive trucks.
They all breed with bully girls with orange hair.
The wimps get the good jobs, marry wives
Who believe in manners and potted plants in a row.
In their late twenties over dinner
They remember the bullies. The taste of roast beef
Dies in their sad mouths. Suddenly angry,
They push away their dinner plates
And take up karate. They sweat a lot,
Kick badly, and enjoy bowing before the wrong flag.
Every time they kick they say "oose," "oose,"
Which means in Japanese "wimp," "wimp."

At the Boys Club I have to wonder
About my kids, dirty angels in dirty *gis*,
Mean and loud, snot hot on their
Upper lips, marked with ball-point
Names on their forearms. Most have been held back
In school at least once.
One was run over by a car but lived.
Two have seen dead people. Another has no
Front teeth and when I asked,
"Leroy, when are you going to get your teeth,"
He said that he had already had them.
Our *dojo* is sorrowful. The rain weeps
On the window. The bare walls stink
Of dust and oily hair,
The floor is splintery. Father Murphy
Says we're going to get a new room
With lights and a heater by next fall.
It's fall now. We have to wait a year.
We suffer with cold toes and watch our breath

Because, I tell my kids, Sensei walked through snow.
We can freeze in the meantime,
Pluck out slivers of glass from
Our feet. Our old rug hides everything,
Even blood. Arron once surprised Manuel,
A sweet roundhouse kick that spanked blood from his face.
Blood has its own course. It jumps,
Flamelike, when you're not looking.
It jumped from Manuel's mouth
And turning around I thought it was a red whip
Of licorice. I walked Manuel to the water
Fountain, slimy bath for dry-throated sparrows.

Karate was introduced from Okinawa
To Tokyo in 1922 by Gichin Funakoshi,
At a national exhibition. School officials
And the military raised their brows, impressed.
If my mother had been Japanese, say, the granddaughter
Of Master Funakoshi, she would have
Used karate on me. I was mean. Three crazy
Dogs lived inside me. I was restless,
Full of odd fun, like throwing mud at girls,
Kicking eggplants, jumping from roofs
With my hands pressed to my side
And eyes closed. But she was Mexican,
Not Japanese, and had her own little tricks
To beat the dogs down. Funakoshi
Didn't believe in hurting children.
He himself was not strong but wise and good,
A great walker in his later years. On his walks
He enjoyed hearing karate screams bouncing
Off walls, grunts, the *ichi, ni, san*
Of calisthenics. He enjoyed tea
And calligraphy, Chinese scholarship,
And remembering his youth, which was long,
A careful ant crawling the length of bamboo.

Sometimes you think it's weird that a man
Can drive nails into a board with his palm,
Knock out cows, punch his fingers
Through watermelons. You hate to get hit
And will say anything not to spar:
"Sensei, my toe hurts; Sensei,
my family is not yet born."
He likes this game of mild complaints,
And with hands on hips, stares
At you, that Mexican watermelon
He could punch through. But you spar anyway,
First with the Berkeley women who are all tattoo,
Then the sissy boys, then the Eurasian,
And finally the sensei, who throws that car
On your chest. Air is never so precious
As when you're on the floor. At home
It's another story. You shower, eat planks of meat,
Play with your daughter, the cats,
Hug your wife a hundred times because
You're so happy to be alive,
And when they're not looking throw a kick
At air, and stomp the bed, jump up
And down in a *fumikomi*. You admit
You're a playground kid who never had enough.
Now in your mid-thirties, it's still play,
A game of tag that stings when you're hit,
Sweat, bruises like pieces of the night,
And the apples of muscle in each arm.
Strange that life is half over, gray is marching
In the hair, and you've not had enough.

If you want to kill an uncle,
The ax kick is perfect. Finger pokes
Can blind a stepfather, a quick thrust to the throat
Stops a lot of people from singing.
If you want to scare a mugger,

Scream and run on the balls of your toes.
I prefer to stay home. The backyard flowers
Are blood-red, the irises the color of veins,
The gate knocking in wind is a bone in the knee.
I like working alone in the backyard,
A kicking bag against a post.
Afterwards I collapse in the lounge chair,
Sweat pooling in the few dents between ribs.
Our clouds are the clouds anywhere,
White with the moisture of grass and trees.
Japan is like this, or the Japan of calendars,
Cloud and swish of blue. The apricot has
Shed its boat-shaped leaves. Last week
Our kitten, Cadet, opened its eyes
And fell over. Now it's prancing
With a shiny tail, nose poking rust-colored leaves.
One moment you think, I would like to lunch
With the Pope. In the next you think,
If Funakoshi were alive,
Could he correct my roundhouse?
If he were with you, in the backyard
On your little triangle of lawn, you could ask,
Hey, is this it? Before you could snap out a kick,
He would tell you to shut up, tell you,
It's good to be back—get me a watermelon!
No tricks. You will kneel and balance
A baby watermelon on your head. With a quick strike,
A fist can find the heart of something very good. ✦

THE ASKING ·

That prayers are not answered
Means very little. It's the prayer itself,
A chill from the shoulders. That I ask,
Show Yourself, and in my dreams I see only cars,
Some trees, faces as flat as nickels.
This, too, means very little. It's the asking
And the prayer, the clean moment,
As now. I'm at the Boys Club, a Monday,
Teaching karate. My kids are
Doing jumping jacks in staggered lines.
The yellow hair bounces, the kinked hair stays in place.
They are happy. Sure, they complain about hurt
Fingers. Sure, they fool with their belts
And ask three times if it's today that they spar
Or Wednesday before it's back to kicks and blocks,
Katas over a worn rug. They are kids,
Unused, clear in the eyes,
Their apples of muscle showing on lean bodies.
They are poor. They eat free lunches here,
Sandwiches from a brown bag, milk,
Bananas flecked with sugary spots.
Their telephones are dead. Their televisions
Are wired for snow and little else.
Few have fathers, and the fathers who do come home
Are covered with cement dust.
Once they sit down they can't get up.

I drive home and think that I know these kids.
I shower and think that it's the front snap kick,
The toes back, a twist from the hip,
That they need. And love,
Something like Christ but not Christ.
That will come later, in time.
For now I read, nap, and sit down to eat.
Grace is a long sentence with lots of "ands."
It's linguine with clam sauce, a salad,

French bread and glasses of ice water.
Mariko is happy because a friend came over.
They dressed in each other's clothes
And went to the store for ice cream.
Carolyn is tired. She went to work,
Cooked. After dinner she'll want to be by herself.
To smoke and run a garden hose in our pond.
Mariko and I talk while we eat. Our cats
Look up with beads of water on their faces.
They follow me like sentries
When I take the plates to the sink.
I do the dishes, then lie on the couch
Thumbing through Oyama's *This Is Karate*.
The Japanese must be crazy.
They smash tile with their faces,
Poke fingers through boards, watermelons,
And catch arrows with one hand.
For years I thought Korean style was better.
Now I have second thoughts. The Japanese have this thing
Of throwing their heads into blocks of ice.
They have *ki*, and a rooted stance.
Their kicks are as simple as up and out.
When I lay the book down and close my eyes,
I see my kids in white *gis*, angels sweeping
The karate floor. It's conjecture, and no more.
They need love, Christ but not Christ,
A father with unexpected gifts in one hand,
A glove in the other.

We read in bed, my wife with
A Southern novel and I with a student paper
That begins, "Percy Shelley was a unique man
Who lived in a unique time." I place
It face down and stare at the ceiling. I want an apple
But am too lazy to get up. I read an article
In my wife's *Glamour* magazine

That says, "67 percent of today's teenagers
Say they believe angels exist. Some 42 percent
Of adult Americans say they've had contact
With the dead." People say a lot of things. Ralph Hinckle,
A bus driver from East Lansing, described a near-death
Experience as he lay crushed under a car:

> My heart had this stinging sensation,
> then stopped. . . . Everything was black,
> then I saw this light that was like
> a cone or something. . . then this really
> beautiful light hit me all over
> and I could only think it was God
> saying I was all right, that He
> was going to give me some of His
> light to get me through the last pain.

But maybe it is neither light nor God.
Sometimes I think a red light is a green light,
And rush ahead without looking.
My student believes Shelley was a unique man,
And our daughter is taking bets that vitamin C
Is in the skin of the grape, not the juice.
We say a lot
And know little. Last night I dreamed
About eating, and as far as I know I can't eat
While I'm asleep. Tonight I might dream
About swimming. The same thing there.
I make up water in my head and throw myself in.
Same with Mr. Hinckle. When he blacked out,
He rolled a lot of light inside his head, scared
Himself, and called it God.
We often call people by the wrong name,
Blend into the wrong off-ramps,
And stare at chicken drumsticks in our refrigerators,
Not knowing why we're there.

My wife is turning pages of her novel.
I have nothing to do but pick up
That student paper. I read once again about Shelley,
That unique man who lived in a unique time.
Lucky for him. And lucky for me that I asked
Another what I should do with my free hours.
I think of my kids, who are in bed, or should be,
And pray for them. Their *gis* are white,
And from any hazy distance
They could be
Fallen angels jumping from heaven. ✦

THE FAMILY IN SPRING ·

Family won't go away. I keep pulling up to them,
Brown faces inside a steamy station wagon.
When I was a boy my uncle flipped pennies
And let me lose, then gave them to me,
Small pile with no sack. I've done the same.
At my nephew's first communion party
I let him close his eyes and choose three times
From my wallet. Two singles is what he got, and a five.
I like my nephew. He missed the twenty and ten.
I talked with my mother, who is like those pennies
And bills, bitter with the acid of fingers.
Grandma is ill, she told me three times.
I told her I was doing OK only once.
I told her I had gone to New York. Carolyn
And I had painted the hallway
And put up new curtains. The cat ran
Away and our second car, the Chevy, was up on blocks.
This was a son speaking to his mother,
Son with the stilts of childhood not pulled down.
We sat and watched the leaves on a tree,
Fiddled with our napkins. Mariko
Brought me three inches of punch in a paper cup.
We'll turn on each other in smaller company.
I got up to leave. My family said
Their goodbyes at a distance, crushed napkins
In their hands.
And went home to call in the backyard
For our lost kitten. Barney, Spike, Midnight.
We never settled on a name.
Now it was lost, a few houses away
For all we knew. When the cat didn't come,
I looked at the Chevy that was droopy eyed from
A wreck, and slammed the hood shut.
I then took my family to dinner because my nephew
Pulled the wrong bills.

That was last April. The weather then is
Today's weather, blue with some wind and leaves.
April or September, I sometimes think
I'd like to start a new family,
Join a household of three kids, not one.
It's not a matter of love. I'm happy here,
With wife and daughter, and I could
Also be happy elsewhere. I suppose
I want more, and I suppose
I'm wrong in the head. How strange,
But for years I didn't wear my wedding band,
And now it's on my finger, wink of light.
Now I'm noticing rings. It's the left hand,
The wink of gold, that says you're married,
That and the two kids in the car,
And the car itself, which is plain,
Or if not plain, then the color white.
A few weeks ago at Safeway I watched a woman
Write out a check for a great pile of groceries.
The wink was there, and a daughter, maybe thirteen,
A little older perhaps, with just enough
Purple dye in her hair to make her OK at school.
I bought my tuna, milk, and a head of lettuce,
And hurried out in time to see them pull away.
The car was a plain white Honda.
Even in the parking lot, the woman's eyes
Were on the dashboard, careful about going too fast.

My wife is a Japanese Methodist.
I went on a retreat with her only last Saturday
Where the woman in the white Honda showed up.
Her ring finger winked a star of gold.
When everyone's finger winked,
I knew I was in the right place. We ate
A lot, sat in lounge chairs, talked baseball scores.

No one complained. No one talked out of line,
Drank too much, or bragged. I liked these people.
They were kind and good, and sensible.
I thought, The one with the white Honda
Is nicer than me. All of them are nicer than me.
For a moment I felt a glow inside,
The blush of happiness with my second beer,
And was helping with the barbecue when I began
To realize that I would never be
As nice as they. This disturbed me,
That they were nicer and didn't care
How much better they were than me.
I joined my wife who was sitting
On the lounge chair. I ate my potato salad
And looked around for a place to throw my ribs.
Guilt, then repentance, is one way to Heaven.
It's Catholic, I suppose. You have one bad thought,
Then another, and suddenly you're in the confessional
Starting over on your knees. I ate my potato salad,
Tried to like them. The Japanese are the people
Who'll get everything the second time around.
I joined the game of volleyball on a new lawn.
I was smiling too much, too little, then not at all. ✦

BROTHER, SISTER, BROTHER ·

Family at one time was a dowry
And a plot of land. Now it's a Christmas card.
A phone call in the night, a mother with
A voodoo doll on a mad sewing machine.
My brother visited last week
To see a baseball game. By the fifth inning
I was drunk and either team could have been winners.
At home we made a fire from wreaths
Of newspapers, had more beers,
Talked money. It's lucky that my brother
Won $25,000 in the California lottery.
All his life he's gotten Cs in school,
Broken arms, and stood under trees that let go
Pine cones that have hurt him. He was
Drinking the night he walked into
A corner market to buy beer.
He and a friend pitched quarters together,
And won. The owner of the market,
Who was as happy as they — young guys
On a Sunday drunk — took their pictures
With a Polaroid, wrote, Money Winners,
And taped it next to the guy in a flannel shirt
Holding up a ten-pound trout. Money has more meaning
Than a trout when you're twenty-three.
When the check came, my brother spent some
And saved a lot. He bought shares
In a transmission company. We talked
About this company, then transmissions,
And never before had I known so much about gears.
The next morning I didn't feel good.
My brother didn't wake up until eleven.
He peed, drank water, and stopped me in the hallway
To take back his words about transmissions.

I'm full of suggestions when my sister asks about men.
There was Ray, a little heavy, a little poor,
With no debts and an almost-new car.
My sister turned the page of the newspaper
And didn't look up to say, No way.
I told her, He's nice, and she told me back,
Everyone is nice but not everyone's rich.
My sister wants a little comfort in her life.
For thirteen years she's been that person
On the other end of the line who answers,
Directory assistance. How may I help you?
Once when I called the operator, I got my sister.
I asked, Debbie, is that you?
She asked back, Gary, what are you doing
On the line? I need a number, I said,
And said I had just finished boxing with her older boy,
Three rounds in my backyard.
She gave me the number
And told me to tell Gerald (her older boy)
To take the hamburger from the freezer.
She called me a bum for having free time
And hung up before I got to ask again about Ray,
Who took her on a walk on a lovely street
And bought her a milk shake and a magazine.
Ray, nice guy with no money, poor dresser without a belt
And in lousy shoes, never had a chance.
Sister wants a fast car,
And a house with glass on the south side,
Warmth like a presence but not quite a presence.
Love is what you want, I tell her at the kitchen table.
And without looking up from her magazine,
She tells me, Shut up.
Which I do.

Sometimes I invite my older brother over.
He is tall, rich. His second wife looks like his first,
Which makes me not want to say too much
Because I will confuse her name
And bring up another time.
I look at my brother a lot,
Ask things like, Is Mom still mad?
Is your car blue, or is that a new one
In the driveway? He says that his new wife
Likes my wife, and I say that everyone
Likes Carolyn. We sip beers
And look at one another. We agree
That Carolyn is nice, and that we'll eat
Fish for dinner. My brother likes fish
And scolding slow waiters.
I often wonder if it's a sin
Not to say something to my brother,
To say with one hand on his shoulder,
For Christ's sake, leave people alone.
The waiter is busy. Sure enough
At the restaurant he stares a big hole into the hostess.
I want to tell him, Relax. It doesn't matter
If people are eating and we're standing up.
After the check is paid, they'll be
Standing up and we'll be sitting down.
Get what I mean, brother?
But I don't say anything. Carolyn and I
Huddle together, arm in arm, and my brother
Wises up and huddles with his new wife,
Whom I can hardly look at because
Any minute I'll call her by that first wife's name
And the swordfish we'll order won't taste right.
Finally we're seated. My brother

Is happy. "Under My Thumb" is on
The loudspeaker, a song he remembers
And I remember because my brother
Had more clothes that fall when the song was a hit:
He picked grapes and I stayed home racing
Our baby brother in a stroller through warm puddles.
We order a carafe of wine,
Toast ourselves, and trade stories about parking tickets —
The dead man slouched at his wheel
And a ticket flapping like wings
Under the wiper blade. When the waiter arrives
With a tray, we stop talking to make room
For the dishes. I take two sips
From my wine, and unfold my napkin.
When I look down, a suspicious fish
Is staring at my fork. The other eye
Is facing its bed of lettuce. I say,
Looks good, and my brother says,
Mine looks good too. Our dressed-up wives,
Ignoring us, fit tomato slices
Into their mouths. It's family when you make
Small talk, drink, and then ask the other
To round off his income in one breath. ✦

A SUNDAY ·

That the flesh should go on now seems to matter.
And goodness in the meantime. I'm trying
To be like others in the church. Katie
Says it's possible, even at this corner,
Leavenworth and Bush, drab men in three sweaters,
Bum on his beat between a boarded-up grocery
And hell. The poor guy has had it. We walk by,
Katie first, then me, and we're all glances.
Maybe that helps, sympathy at a distance.
I know two prayers almost by heart.
Money would help too, but I feel odd
Floating down a dollar. Katie would see me,
Think, It doesn't help. She would be right
Of course, and all day I would think, A dollar
Doesn't help. Two dollars, three,
Three and some change.
We're cold enough to walk by.
At Katie's apartment we need two keys
To get in. We shudder, undo our coats,
And warm our hands with coffee.
We play backgammon, listen to music,
And butter bagels—sesame seeds on all fingers.
The grapes are old, and we throw them away.
She's showing me a photograph of herself,
Then nineteen and with long hair.
When the phone rings—it's her recently married sister.
She's fine, I gather from their talk.
She's bought a new coat, place mats,
Exchanged a lamp for a clock radio. Roger,
Her husband, bought her slippers, and sold the boat.
Katie is happy. The lines around her mouth
Deepen as she talks. More lines
On her forehead when she laughs.
She hangs up and says it was her sister
And her sister says Hi.

I like Katie. There's not much to say.
We play backgammon, and neither of us minds losing.
We smile at our losses
And stare out the windows, five flights up
Where pigeons huddle under the shadow-dark eaves.
At this height people don't mind
Being looked at. The shades are up.
The kitchens yellow with light.
The Chinese man in his undershirt is at the stove,
Now at the refrigerator, now at the stove.
The woman directly across from us
Is watching television. Light flickers
Like someone shuffling cards. On a quiet Sunday
Men come and go in their pajamas and purple robes.
Katie puts on a kettle of water.
I thumb through a magazine:
Life seems more real in pictures, and happier.
I want to ask about God, but don't know how.
Katie doesn't know how either. A small, thin cross
Hides behind her top button, sparkles sometimes
When she turns or bends to slip into a shoe.
God troubles me with the same questions.
I want very badly to know how to talk about Christ.
Others seem to know. Katie's friends can run
A finger through the Bible and each chapter,
Some verses. The pot of water comes to a boil.
We lean against the countertop in the kitchen.
God is someone who is with you,
Like now, she says.

The small hours of Sunday gather in the shadows.
I leave Katie running water
In the bathroom sink. You can't see,
She says, and closes the door behind her.
You're married, and should know better.

That's true. I think about this as I drive home.
I've been married twelve years, nearly thirteen,
And running water in the bathroom sink
Is a womanly thing. Panty hose
Drip in the shower. Bras drip too
But slower, large drops from secret niches.
When I pull into the driveway,
My wife is watering the begonias.
I take the hose from her hand and drink,
Then pat her hip and say I'm home,
I'm almost hungry. She asks me how Mass was.
I say fine. The priest was looking at me
When he spoke about sin. She raises her eyebrows
And says, He knows his parish.
Before we go in she shows me
Where an arbor should go.
I look at the ground and try to find
Something to say. I want my wife to like me.
I look up to a homing pigeon cooing
On the neighbor's fence. We call Mariko,
Our daughter, who comes out of the house
With a book in her hand. That's a homing pigeon,
I point. You see the band on its leg?
We forget about the arbor. We go inside.
Dinner is what we had last night,
Cabbage rolls and a salad. After dinner Mariko
And I play chess. She's nine but smart.
Both of us feel cocky, but ten moves into the game
We're serious. It's different from
Playing with Katie, who wants my company.
Mariko wants my money, a dollar to her polished dime.
Since I'm a kind fool with dead bishops,
I lose. I shower, and in the shower I sing
A Christian hymn. It's not that I feel that close
To Christ, it's that I like the music.

Most of the words are *Holy, Holy, Hallelujah*,
And plenty of *forevers*.

                    Sunday nights,
With the dishes done and put away,
My wife and I usually dance. That is,
After we're bathed and in robes,
We dance to oldies on the radio.
My daughter's favorite is Sam Cooke's
"Twisting the Night Away." That's about what
She does, twists until fifteen to nine,
Then it's bed and a few pages from a library book.
But tonight I feel OK just to sit on the couch
And read the travel section in
The newspaper. My daughter
Is speaking pig Latin. *Ello-hay ad-day.*
Anks-thay or-fay e-thay ive-fay ollars-day.
It's from a book she's read,
A book that shouldn't have been written
Because she won't be quiet. When she starts
Isten-lay up-way, I shush her and pat my lap.
We read about Annecy in Southern France,
A place that looks like France.
It's canals and old buildings and shoppers
Handling fruit at rickety stands. The writer says,
"Thrust in the center of the Thiou,
The exquisite 12th-century Palais de l'Ile seemed to
Cut the water like the prow of a dream ship."
The larger the paper, the more the travel writer
Feels for his readers. What man was
Ever so lucky as to throw a newspaper onto
The floor and have his daughter understand?
I bounce her off my knee. Then it's *ood-gay ight-nay.*
Which is to say, Goodnight,
But with a hug and a crazy kiss.

On Monday my students will show me panties
When they uncross their legs—pink, white,
Pinkish white. I'm at the blackboard holding
A piece of chalk. This scares me,
The panties I mean, because I want to say
Something smart with the chalk,
That "each of them are handsome" is wrong,
That a period goes inside quotation marks.
I want to be nice of course, and Catholic,
But not so Catholic that I can't at least glance,
Smile inwardly. Once the chalk rolled from my palm
And I didn't dare bend to get it
Because I might see more, or nothing, just black.
The class looked at the chalk.
And I looked at the class, said, Let's go home.
That day I was happy. I bought my wife a magazine.
I got myself a Southern novel about how nothing fits,
Hats or shoes, and the false teeth of bluish Negroes.
That was months ago. My wife has a new magazine
And I'm reading about a red mountain lion.
It's Sunday, late, and our daughter is in bed.
We're in bed as well. Two moths
Are beating our yellowish lampshade.
An ant is hiding in the folds of an apricot pit.
I have worn Sunday to its end. I like Katie,
And love my wife and daughter,
And believe a dirty face
Is the same as a washed one to God.
I'm going to be like others in the church
And good in the meantime. I close my eyes.
Breathe in and breathe out, and think
Of all the chalk that has ever slipped from my palm.
Chalk that picks up black when it rolls away.
It won't happen again, or if it does, I won't look
To see if it's pink or white, or pinkish white. ◆

MY EVENINGS OUT ·

Three years ago it was the house-remodeling course
At the navy base in Oakland. I was smart enough
Then to memorize the standard length of screws,
To write in a notebook. Snails can eat paint.
They're the color of your house when you step on them—
Yellow froth, a green or a gray. I forgot about foundations,
Window sashes and oil-based paints, floors,
But am almost certain that a ¾-inch bit can vent a house.
Like us, a house needs to breathe in every kind
Of weather, and spring is when the winged termites
Can start their holes if you're not careful.
I stayed three class meetings.
The fourth week, I said goodbye to wife and daughter,
And went to the bookstore and read not in the Bible
But in *The Catholic Worker*, "What you do for
The least of us, you do to me."
When I returned home, my wife was doing push-ups—
Her evening exercise on the living room rug.
She stopped to ask about class. I said it was fine.
I said that oil-based paints are all the same.
If a floor squeaks, nail it. If a roof leaks,
The hole is not where you think.
She turned onto her back for sit-ups,
And asked, How is that going to make our kitchen better?

I took Japanese. I stayed only one class.
The teacher kept asking for dimes
Each time she handed out copies of Xeroxed
Material. It was funny. She would finish
With one exercise, and then go up
And down the rows, saying, Exact change, please.
I took Spanish and Italian, and Impressionist Art
In the fall, which made me sleepy. Not the art
But the meeting time of 7:30 to 10:00 and the terrible chairs.
I remembered the biography of a poet
Who said, The greatest thing in America
Is Europe. Native Americans of course
Would think otherwise. I thought of

This line when we studied van Gogh,
And remembered a girlfriend who lost the tip
Of her finger in a mower. That didn't stop her
From becoming the first "milkperson" in Fresno.
I remembered being jealous—
Sue in the *Fresno Bee*, and me, a college student,
Still weeding flower beds for my money.
That was years ago. I'm almost happy
Where I am, and Sue, I understand, pulls horse trailers
Through the foothills for a living.

I stayed three class meetings
Before it was back to the bookstore
Where I looked through atlases. I want to travel,
And have admired China and Singapore
And would go except I like sleeping in my own bed.
At a sale table I read pages from a book on miracles.
Relatives show up when they're dead and not before,
Like Uncle who was green, my brother said,
A little more than light but not quite flesh.
Or even Father who had this habit of coming back
To the old house just as my uncle (a live one)
Got into the tub. Uncle would listen, a bar of soap
In his hand, and listen. Water has one kind of sound,
And the dead another, something like gravel
My uncle said. Gravel spread thickly
Around the pond, dark water with its own wind.
Uncle said that he was scared the first time,
Nighttime in a tub of water,
Moths beating the light bulb and the towels falling
From their racks. Now he sits in bathwater in West Covina,
A little black in the lungs, arms stained from work.
I thought of Uncle as I thumbed through this book
On miracles, then left to drink a soda
Outside the bookstore. The book display
Was done right. Three flies
Crawled over a new novel by John Updike.

Now I sweat a lot. *Doshinkan karatedo* looked easy
When I first watched. Renshi seemed strong
But not so strong as to throw his face into tiles.
Easy, I thought, and did thirty push-ups on my knuckles.
I looked up. The clock was washing its face
With a long black hand. More red knuckles,
Some sit-ups on folding chairs, squats—
Spider of time on the karate floor.
One month, twelve classes,
And what concerns me is a *tettsui*,
A wrist strike shaped like a chicken's head.
I asked, Won't I break my wrist?
Renshi said, No, if it's like this.
And palsied his wrist and hand into a chicken head.
He says no a lot,
And I think a lot when I kick.
In two months I may be gone. Aikido has its falls
And grabs, and a clean *dojo* of calligraphy
And white walls, *shoji* screen with its snowy light.
I like their black skirts, the wooden tiles
With your name burned in Japanese,
And that the students are generally clean—
No toenails or rinds of dead skin
Pressed in your palm when you get up from a fall.
That's later. Now I'm in a karate class.
After class I will consider the remaindered books
At a wobbly table at Pegasus Books.
A troubled writer has a lot to say. The books climb
To the ceiling, and patrons can climb as well
On the kind of aluminum ladders painters use.
I walk between tables, leave, and drive home.
My wife is sweaty from her workout,
My daughter smart from the three books in her lap.
We invent misery for our bodies,
Then our minds, and then, having nothing else to do,
Look for ways to make it stop. ✦

Books by Gary Soto

Home Course in Religion
A Summer Life
Baseball in April
Who Will Know Us?
A Fire in My Hands
California Childhood
Lesser Evils
Small Faces
Living Up the Street
Black Hair
Where Sparrows Work Hard
The Tale of Sunlight
The Elements of San Joaquin

This book was typeset by

On Line Typography, San Francisco

Book design by

Nancy Brescia

Cover illustration and design by

Alex Laurant